The ethics you live out as you go about your work can

provide the foundation for excellence.

The high caliber organization is, after all, merely

a reflection of its people.

The Ethics
of Excellence

Price Pritchett, Ph.D.

Excellence never happens
by accident.

We have to *make* it happen.
And our methods
matter every bit as much as
our results.

Excellence is a process, not just an outcome.

Sure, we have to hold out for high standards in the products or services we provide. The goods must be more than "good enough." But so must our approach — you know, our methodology, the way we do business and deal with people. How could the *ends* be considered excellent if we can't be proud of the *means*?

Excellence calls for character . . . integrity . . . fairness . . . honesty . . . a determination to do what's right. High ethical standards, across the board.

We can't achieve excellence through talent alone. Or merely by making technological improvements. We can't even buy our way to excellence, no matter how much money we have available to spend. More dollars will never do it.

We have to develop a strong corporate conscience. Ethical muscle. And that doesn't happen by accident either.

The only way we can develop muscle is through regular exercise. As soon as we stop stretching and working toward higher ethics, our standards start to sag. The muscle gets soft, and instead of excellence we have to settle for mediocrity. Maybe something even worse.

The question is, when so many others cut corners, shave the truth, self-deal, believe in the fast buck, and follow the crowd along the low road of least resistance, can we even *afford* to travel the high road of ethical behavior?

Frankly, we can't afford anything else.

Any other competitive angle is a pure crapshoot in today's business world. Companies with shaky ethics and shabby standards will be crippled as they try to compete in our changing world.

We need timeless principles to steer by in running our organizations and building our personal careers. We need high standards . . . the ethics of excellence.

ISBN 978-0-944002-09-4

PRITCHETT

The Ethics of Excellence

You weren't born ethical.

Every one of us had to start with nothing. Zero ethics. Born innocent, "pure as the driven snow," we had a grace period — a couple of years or so — free of any social standards regarding moral duty and ethical conduct.

Very soon, though, other people came to expect more of us. We were taught right from wrong . . . good from bad. We were rewarded for being responsible and punished for being irresponsible. The world began to hold us accountable for our behavior.

But the ethics of excellence were a long way off. We started out empty-handed, without even a conscience. Then, to make matters worse, we had some poor teachers along the way. You know, lousy role models.

In some cases our teachers meant well, maybe even taught okay, yet we fouled up as students. How many lessons of life did we misunderstand? How often did we draw the wrong conclusions?

As kids we often were rewarded for doing the wrong things. After all, the school of life doesn't offer a fool-proof curriculum. We found ways to work the system, discovering that what *works* isn't always what's *right*. In fact, life quickly taught us that behaving ethically and right could be painful. Who among us wasn't punished by parents for telling the truth about our childhood crimes?

Before we hit kindergarten we were practiced in the art of lying. Dealing with other kids in the family or down the street, we honed our selfish instincts, grabbing for the best toys and taking more than our share of cookies. By the age of three we knew how to shrewdly manipulate, playing both ends (mommy and daddy) against the middle.

We all faced painful ethical challenges before we even knew how to spell our names. There were tough choices. Tradeoffs. Confusing signals regarding how to live one's life.

And here we are now, today, still struggling. Still trying to sort things out. Still trying to work our way through life effectively.

About the only thing that has changed is the scope of the problem. There's more at stake now. And we're in a position, as grownups, to do a lot more — good or bad — for ourselves, our organization, our world.

But we still must wrestle with our imperfect ethics.

A code for the road.

Some years ago Crosby, Stills & Nash sang a hit song about ethics — about life and influence and moral development. They pointed out the need for standards of conduct:

"You, who are on the road, must have a code
That you can live by —" *

You'll find universal agreement on the value of a behavior code, on the need for some sort of ethical system. Even the crooks count on "honor among thieves," and countries actually wage war according to certain rules. On the job, and in the rest of our day-to-day living, we each need a "code for the road."

Organizations often draw up a credo or code of conduct explaining what the company believes in, specifying the do's and don'ts, and highlighting the ethical challenges most likely to come along. We need that.

This book offers coaching along more general lines.

No matter what our job, no matter what kind of organization we're part of, the following guidelines will help us achieve the ethics of excellence.

Obey the law . . .
but don't hide behind it.

Start here: Live by the law of the land.

Trouble is, of course, there aren't laws for everything. And sometimes people hide behind laws to do their dirty deeds. You could get away with a lot of ugly stuff without ever being fined or sent to jail.

Even if you go beyond the *letter* of the law, and live by its spirit and intent, the organization can fall far short of excellence. The legal system doesn't always serve as a good guide for your conscience. You can step way over the ethical line and still be inside the law.

The same thing goes for rules, policies, and procedures — you know, the organization's "internal laws." You can "go by the book" and still behave unethically. Still not move beyond mediocrity.

High standards — the ethics of excellence — come to life through your basic values, your character, integrity, and honesty.

Obeying the law is the bare minimum. It's only the first step toward high standards.

Do the right thing
when there is such a thing.

You have to remember that people look at things differently. We don't all see things the same way, so we won't all agree on what the right thing is.

We can't even count on "the right thing" to be fixed, static, or necessarily absolute. The line between right and wrong often gets fuzzy. Watch how it moves. What's right in one situation might be wrong in the next. What's good in some respects can be bad in others. Sometimes the situation is so complicated that you have trouble just figuring out what the right thing is. And even the right thing can be done wrong.

Circumstances often corner you, too, leaving no option but to settle for "semi-right." Or maybe your only choice is to pick the best from a bunch of bad alternatives.

When you *can* make it this simple, though, just do the right thing. Even if you could get away with less. Even when other people are doing the wrong thing. Even though the wrong thing seems like no big deal.

Your ethical muscle grows stronger every time you choose right over wrong.

Listen to your conscience,
although you
can't always trust it.

Pay attention to the voice within. But don't believe everything you hear.

People's consciences vary as much as their personalities. Some have inner voices that scream, while others hear only a whisper. Your conscience may bully you, or it might be lazy. Certainly some people feel guilt far more than others. One person can be cruel, wicked, and dishonest, without feeling any pangs of conscience. The next person can suffer heavy guilt for committing trivial wrongs.

Sometimes the voice of your conscience gets drowned out by crowd noise or by the pep rally of temptations. And your mind may put some selfish spin on the ball, rationalizing that it's okay to veer away from the ethical route. When we run into conflicts between ethical "shoulds" and our selfish "wants," we all figure out ways to con our conscience.

Bottom line? The conscience is a fairly unreliable guide for moral behavior. But take pains to listen, because it has your best interests at heart.

Talk it out with others . . .
but choose your others
carefully.

You've given some "air time" to your conscience . . . now get a second opinion. Find someone else to serve as a sounding board. But choose carefully.

Some people are lousy advisors — long on talk and short on sense. Their free advice may be worth no more than it costs. And someone speaking gently with solid advice may not be heard over another person who has strong lungs, but weak judgment.

The best bet is to discuss the matter with people whose ethics you admire — those you respect for their honesty, fairness, and integrity. And try to talk things over with people who hold an opposing point of view, or who look at the situation from a different angle. Don't just rely on whomever is handy or some "yes man" who would never challenge your thinking.

If you look around long enough, of course, you can always find someone who will tell you what you want to hear.

That's not the idea. Find people who'll tell you what you need to hear.

Prepare to be punished
for honesty.

When you hold out for high standards, people are impressed — but they don't always like you for it. Not everybody will be on your side in your struggle to do what's right and ethical.

In fact, sometimes even *you* won't be on your side. You'll wrestle with inner conflict, torn between what you should do and what you want to do.

You'll also aggravate other people. Seems when you walk the straight and narrow you always step on someone's toes. Don't count on the ethics of excellence to make you popular with everyone.

Even "the system" won't always be on your side. Organizations, like parents, don't always reward the right things. Deliberately or inadvertently, the organization may reinforce unethical stuff and punish people who act with integrity.

Excellence doesn't come free. We all pick up some battle scars on the road to high standards.

Stay out of ethical debt.

Think long-term, not short-term, as you make your ethical choices.

Carefully weigh the appeal of today's temptations against the punishment they could cause later. If you sell out your high standards in order to get immediate goodies, you can end up deep in "ethical debt."

The ethics of excellence require a sense of perspective. Look at the big picture. If you live for the moment, do you mortgage the future? What happens if you put your reputation at risk . . . and lose the bet? If you're unwilling to defer pleasure or endure some "pain" for now, are you likely to end up later deep in the hole?

Eventually, we have to "settle up" and pay the price for our ethical violations. Just remember the old line that says, "You can pay me now . . . or you can pay me later." Often you can buy some time, but when you "pay later" you'll probably have to pay more.

When today offers you a short-term payoff for ethical shortcuts, consider the long-term costs.

As tough as it sometimes looks on the front end, it's easier to do right than undo wrong.

Sweat the small stuff.

How can we be trusted with big things if we're not trustworthy with things that are small?

In the ethics of excellence, everything you do counts. The most minor violations weaken your reputation for rightness. As Tom Peters says in *Thriving on Chaos*, "Integrity may be about little things as much or more than big ones."

Let your character be revealed in the small stuff, so others come to see you (and so you come to see yourself) as one who acts ethically in all things. Any violation of honesty and integrity, however small, dilutes your ethical strength, leaving you weaker for the big challenges you're bound to face sooner or later.

The simple question is: Where will you draw the line?

Don't allow your finer instincts to become a casualty of the little everyday crimes of ethical compromise.

High standards leave no room for mushy morals.

React to smells.

Ethical dilemmas have a way of sneaking up on a person. From a distance they can look pretty harmless, even though you pick up the scent of something wrong. But if you wait for trouble to come close enough for you to see it clearly, the bad smell may already be rubbing off on you.

The ethics of excellence call for good defensive moves — for prevention, preferably, rather than cure. Instead of waiting for hard proof that you're dabbling with something dishonest or dishonorable, pay attention to symptoms. Keep a safe distance from things that raise your suspicion. Unless, of course, instead of giving trouble a wide berth, you need to attack.

But don't let yourself be cornered by waiting too long to deal with the situation. Think ahead. Pay attention to what's coming. Anticipate trouble, and give yourself enough lead time to deal effectively with ethical traps.

If something smells funny, stay away from it. Or help get rid of it.

Be a cheerleader for
ethical champions.

When you see people with "the right stuff," those who choose right over wrong or "iffy," let them know you're proud of them.

Showcase the people who fight for high standards. Spread the word about others' good deeds. Tell the stories about the organization's ethical champions who push it toward excellence. Do your part to make sure that people get credit for acting with integrity, particularly when facing tough choices.

People often worry that taking an ethical stand could hurt their careers. It takes nerve, commitment — real guts — to tackle so many of today's moral problems.

Encourage the courageous, so they'll have the will to carry on.

Permit mistakes so you don't promote coverups.

Everybody makes honest mistakes, but there's no such thing as an honest cover-up.

Give people, *including yourself,* clear permission to make mistakes. Disallowing honest foul-ups has a way of forcing lies. People commit an ethical violation in an effort to cover their tracks. The result proves that ethical violations are self-reproducing. They feed on themselves.

The threat of disapproval and punishment for flawed behavior makes a person wish for an escape route. The idea of hiding mistakes is seductive, and the carrot of the cover-up dangles as an appealing solution. But the best approach is to level with others, to go public with what was done wrong.

Honesty saves energy and attention for fixing the problem, instead of spending it on hiding things. Plus, a cover-up just doubles a person's vulnerability — somebody still might discover the mistake, and also find one guilty of deception. Twice the trouble.

Since nobody's perfect, mistakes should be allowed. Cover-ups shouldn't.

Mind more than your
own business.

High *personal* standards aren't enough for organizational excellence. You've got to be intolerant of low standards in *others.*

Part of your job is to help set, promote, and enforce the ethics of excellence. Whether you like it or not, you will be one of the architects of the corporate conscience. For good or for bad, you help build the character of the company. This is not — cannot be — just the job of top management. If you work here, it's *your* job.

Make it clear that you expect nothing less than high ethical standards from coworkers, clients and customers, vendors, and — to the extent possible — even your competitors.

If you accommodate questionable practices in others who touch your organization, you risk soiling its reputation.

Anybody whose hands aren't clean can get the place dirty.

Learn to live with
shades of gray.

Right and wrong is not a two-toned picture. Many of the ethical issues you encounter are fuzzy and blurred. Instead of being free to choose good or bad, you have to work through a hazy fog of half-tones.

Prepare yourself for this kind of ethical uncertainty, because life throws you into predicaments where you have to make judgment calls. Tradeoffs and compromises. Instead of selecting from two clear-cut categories — one right, one wrong — you often face multiple options. All problematic, none perfect.

What's right or fair or moral gets to be highly controversial. You need to accept the fact that you can't keep everybody happy.

And here's a key point: Everyone else wrestles with these same kinds of conflict. If they happen to make a call that doesn't serve your best interests, that doesn't mean they're unethical. Sooner or later in life, each of us is a victim of circumstances. It's not fair to scream "foul" just because you don't get your way.

Painful choices usually make all parties feel bad. Even if everyone lived by high ethical standards, it wouldn't keep people from getting hurt.

Bear the blame for
your behavior.

You can't put someone else in charge of your morals. Ethics is a personal discipline.

Sure, you'll find a well-coordinated *group* effort in organizations that are known for excellence. But, ultimately, ethics ends up an individual exercise. You have to get beyond blaming others . . . give up your excuses . . . stand responsible for what you do. High standards start to sag when people try to delegate accountability for their personal character and integrity.

Maybe you're tempted to put your reputation in the hands of higher authorities — such as bosses, experts, or some other big shots — wanting them to take the rap if you do something out of line. If your excuse is, "I was just following orders," that's passing the buck upward.

If you give in to "group think" — bend to the pressure of mob ethics — you're trying to excuse your behavior by losing your face in the crowd. "Everybody does it" is a cop-out, one more way of trying to dodge blame for what *you* decided to do.

Finally, saying that you're merely "getting even" doesn't get you off the hook. Revenge, using somebody else's unethical behavior as justification for your own, is just another way of trying to shift the blame for your behavior.

No more finger-pointing. The ethical monkey rides on your back.

Let pride be your guide.

Live according to the ethics of excellence, and you can always stand proud.

Here's a test you can run: If what you're thinking about doing made the evening news in your hometown, how would you look? Would you be pleased to see your story on page one of the local paper? Would you mind having your actions analyzed on "20/20"?

Let's make it even more personal. Would you care if your children knew about it? Or your parents?

If the threat of exposure to public scrutiny makes you squirm, then your pride is saying something important. Pay attention. You're playing with something that could tarnish a reputation — yours *and* the organization's.

Pride — not vanity, but dignity and self-respect — should carry a lot of weight in helping you make up your mind. Let pride help you decide.

Don't *say* what you believe
about ethics . . .
show what you believe.

The ethics of excellence are grounded in *action* — what you actually do, rather than what you say you believe. Talk, as the saying goes, is cheap. Or as Adlai Stevenson put it, "It is often easier to fight for principles than to live up to them."

People really won't show much faith in the claims you make about your personal standards. But they pay close attention to what you do. Particularly when temptation grows sweetest. Or when your moral standards come under heavy fire.

Anyone can do right when it's easy. But the ethical hero hangs in there when it's hard. Your personal ethics, and the organization's value system, are best revealed under stress. When the heat is on, you show your true character. Everybody watches to see if you "walk your talk."

The organization that preaches one thing and does another is considered hypocritical. Not excellent. Lip service isn't the kind of exercise that builds ethical muscle.

We can't win the struggle for high standards if we just talk a good game . . . we've got to play a good game.

Where the buck stops.

Notice that "I" is at the center of the word "ethical." There is no "they." Achieving the ethics of excellence is our individual assignment. The buck stops here.

We've got to get past the idea that somebody else is supposed to fix things — like "top management," the politicians, our justice system, the schools, or even our religious institutions. These faceless groups don't exist except through the lives, the day-to-day behavior, of common people like you and me.

Who is this vague "they" we blame for so many of our problems? "They" is the obscure party we use as our whipping boy to camouflage the fact that we — you and I and other specific human beings just like us — have to start doing things differently. "They" can't fix anything. We can.

But when we get enough people who don't care, and who don't accept personal responsibility for high ethical standards, our organization gets the "M" disease. *Mediocrity.* Anybody in the place can be a carrier.

By the same token, every individual can carry the cure: The ethics of excellence.

For information regarding PRITCHETT's training, keynotes,
and consulting built around our handbooks, please call **800-992-5922**.

About the Author

Price Pritchett, Chairman & CEO of PRITCHETT, LP, is recognized internationally as a leading authority on merger integration and major organizational change.

His consulting assignments have taken him to the Far East, Europe, the United Kingdom, and all across the Americas. He has been quoted in *Fortune, Business Week, The Wall Street Journal, USA Today,* and most major U.S. city newspapers, and interviewed on CNN, CNBC, as well as numerous corporate cable channels.

He holds a Ph.D. in psychology and has been a consultant to top executives in major corporations for almost three decades. His firm's client list includes 3M, General Electric, IBM, Eastman Kodak, Citibank, Southwest Airlines, Ernst & Young, John Hancock Insurance, American Airlines, BellSouth, SmithKline Beecham, Hewlett-Packard, ExxonMobil and numerous other *Fortune* 1000 companies.

HIS 30 BOOKS AND HANDBOOKS HAVE MORE THAN 20 MILLION COPIES IN PRINT, MAKING HIM ONE OF THE BEST-SELLING BUSINESS AUTHORS IN THE U.S.

The Ethics of Excellence

1-49 copies	_____ copies at $7.95 each
50-99 copies	_____ copies at $7.50 each
100-999 copies	_____ copies at $6.95 each
1,000-4,999 copies	_____ copies at $6.75 each
5,000-9,999 copies	_____ copies at $6.50 each
10,000 or more copies	_____ copies at $6.25 each

Name _____

Job Title _____

Organization _____

Address _____

City, State _____ Zip Code _____

Country _____ Phone _____ Fax _____

Email _____

Purchase order number (if applicable) _____

Applicable sales tax, shipping and handling charges will be added. Prices subject to change.
Orders less than $250 require prepayment.
*Orders of $250 or more may be invoiced.
Standard shipping is FedEx 3-Day unless otherwise specified.

☐ Check Enclosed   ☐ Please Invoice*

☐ **VISA**   ☐ **MasterCard**   ☐ **AMERICAN EXPRESS**

Name on Card _____

Card Number _____ Expiration Date _____

Signature _____ Date _____

TO ORDER
By Phone: 800-992-5922
Online: www.pritchettnet.com
Call for our mailing address or fax number.

PRITCHETT
Dallas, TX